ANDREW LUCK

By Ryan Nagelhout

Gareth Stevens
Publishing

Please visit our website www.garethstevens.com. For a free color catalog of all our high-quality books, call toll free 1-800-542-2595 or fax 1-877-542-2596.

Library of Congress Cataloging-in-Publication Data

Nagelhout, Ryan.
Andrew Luck / by Ryan Nagelhout.
  p. cm. — (Today's great quarterbacks)
Includes index.
ISBN 978-1-4824-0125-7 (pbk.)
ISBN 978-1-4824-0126-4 (6-pack)
ISBN 978-1-4824-0124-0 (library binding)
1. Luck, Andrew, — 1989- — Juvenile literature. 2. Football players — United States — Biography — Juvenile literature. 3. Quarterbacks (Football) — United States — Biography — Juvenile literature. I. Nagelhout, Ryan. II. Title.
GV939.L81 N34 2014
796.332092—dc23

First Edition

Published in 2014 by
Gareth Stevens Publishing
111 East 14th Street, Suite 349
New York, NY 10003

Copyright © 2014 Gareth Stevens Publishing

Designer: Nicholas Domiano
Editor: Ryan Nagelhout

Photo credits: Cover, p. 1 Peter G. Aiken/Getty Images Sport/Getty Images; p. 5 Jason Merritt/Getty Images Entertainment/Getty Images; p. 7 Ezra Shaw/Getty Images Sport/ Getty Images; p. 9 Justin Sullivan/Getty Images Sport/Getty Images; p. 11 Bob Levey/Getty Images Sport/Getty Images; p. 13 Doug Pensinger/Getty Images Sport/Getty Images; p. 15 AP Photo/Aaron M. Sprecher; p. 17 Stephen Dunn/Getty Images Sport/Getty Images; p. 19 Jeff Zelevansky/Getty Images Sport/Getty Images; p. 21 Al Bello/Getty Images Sport/ Getty Images; p. 23 Doug Kapustin/MCT/Getty Images; p. 25 Jonathan Daniel/Getty Images Sport/Getty Images; p. 27 Joe Robbins/Getty Images Sport/Getty Images; p. 29 Jamie McCarthy/Getty Images Entertainment/Getty Images.

Printed in the United States of America

CPSIA compliance information: Batch #CW14GS: For further information contact Gareth Stevens, New York, New York at 1-800-542-2595.

CONTENTS

Meet Andrew

Andrew Luck is a great quarterback! He plays in the **National Football League** (NFL).

Andrew was born September 12, 1989, in Washington, DC. His parents are named Oliver and Kathy.

World Traveler

Andrew grew up all over the world! He lived in England and Germany. He mostly grew up in Houston, Texas.

9

Andrew's dad, Oliver, played football, too! He was a quarterback for the Houston Oilers. Andrew wanted to play football like his dad.

Andrew Luck

Oliver Luck

Houston Hotshot

Andrew's dad was also in charge of

Major League Soccer teams. Andrew

loves to play and watch soccer!

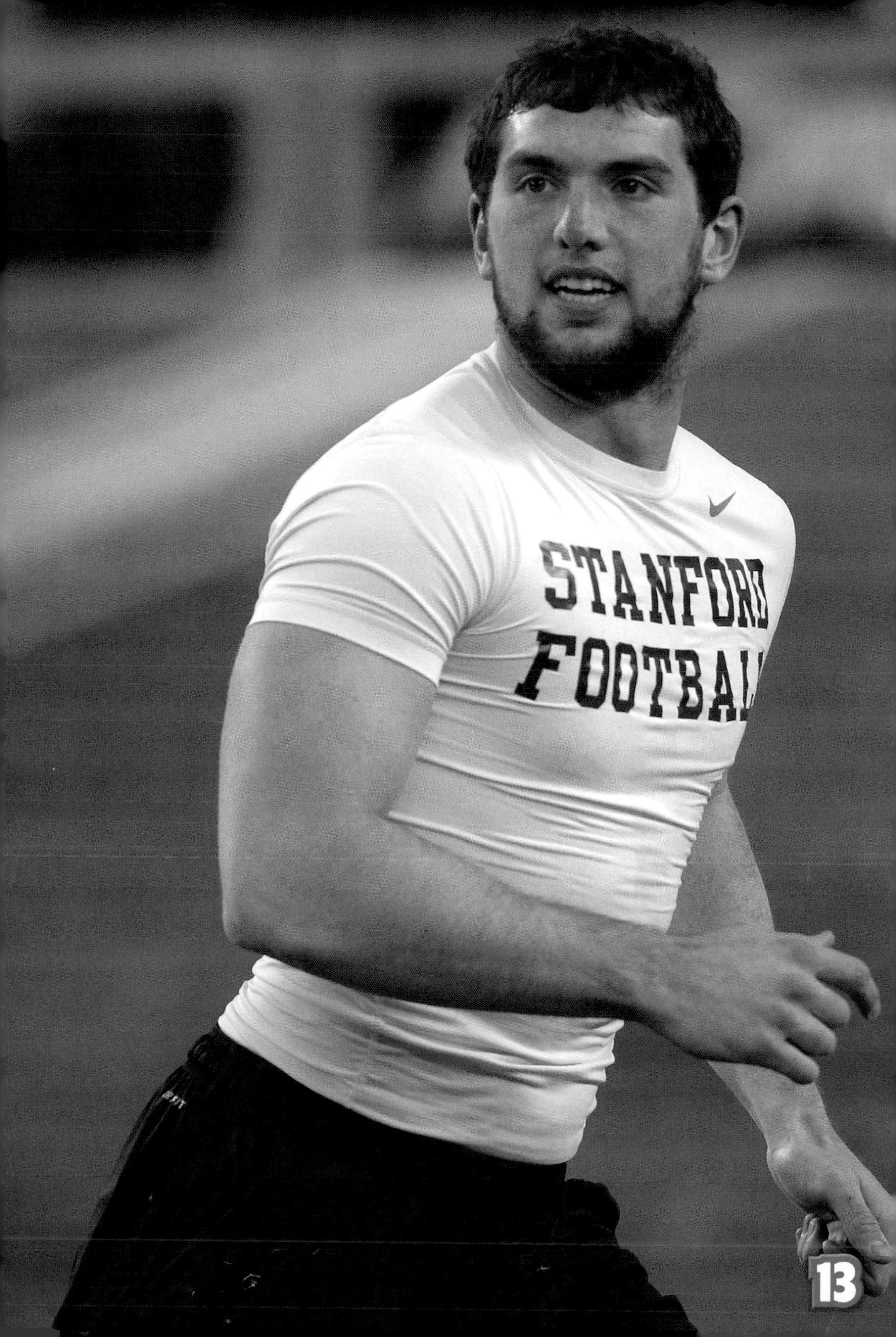
STANFORD
FOOTBALL

Andrew played football in high school. He started at quarterback for 3 years at Stratford High School in Houston. **College** football was next!

15

Stanford Star

Andrew went to Stanford University in California. He started at quarterback for three seasons. Andrew was a star!

17

Andrew was a finalist for the Heisman **Trophy** in 2010 and 2011. This is college football's top honor.

Top Pick

NFL teams thought Andrew was going to be a star. The Indianapolis Colts made him the first overall pick in the 2012 NFL **Draft**.

The Colts released Peyton Manning in 2012. Andrew became the Colts' starting quarterback. He wore number 12, just like he did in college.

Rookie Records

Andrew had a great year in 2012.

He set NFL records for most yards,

attempts, and 300-yard games

for a **rookie**.

The Colts made the playoffs in 2012!

Andrew was the first number 1 overall

draft pick to start a playoff game

as a rookie.

What's Next?

Andrew's career is just getting started.

What will he accomplish next?

Timeline

1989   Andrew is born on September 12.

2004   Andrew starts at quarterback for Stratford High School.

2008   Andrew commits to Stanford University.

2009   Andrew starts at quarterback for the Stanford Cardinals.

2011   Andrew earns his second Heisman Trophy nomination.

2012   Indianapolis Colts draft Andrew first overall in the NFL Draft.

        Andrew breaks three NFL records in his first season.

2013   Andrew starts a playoff game as a rookie.

Books

Fishman, Jon M. *Andrew Luck*. Minneapolis, MN: Lerner Publications, 2014.

O'Neal, Claire. *Andrew Luck*. Hockessin, DE: Mitchell Lane Publishers, 2014.

Websites

Andrew Luck's NFL Player Page

nfl.com/player/andrewluck/2533031/profile
See Andrew's stats, video highlights, and more on this site.

Official Indianapolis Colts Website

colts.com
Find out more about the Colts from their official team page.

Glossary

college: a school after high school

draft: a way to pick new football players for the NFL

Major League Soccer: a professional soccer league in the United States and Canada

National Football League: the top football league in the United States

rookie: a first-year player in professional sports

trophy: a prize given for winning or doing something

Index